C000259926

Cults
A practical
guide

by Ian Haworth

Published by the Cult Information Centre (UK)

Dedicated to Anna Walker

1911 - 2000

Friend, supporter, tireless worker and fund-raiser for CIC

Cults: A practical guide
© Ian Haworth/Cult Information Centre 2001
Reprinted 2006, 2008 (with revisions)

Cult Information Centre (CIC)
BCM Cults, London WC1N 3XX
Tel: 0845 4500 868
www.cultinformation.org.uk

ISBN: 1-873166-84-2

Printed in the UK

Contents

About this Booklet

I had the idea for this booklet in the mid 1980s when I prepared my first outline of it. However, such is the overwhelming workload for a full-time specialist in cultism that the actual writing was put on hold until 1999, when I finally shelved other projects in order to create the time for its completion.

The booklet is designed to be a summary of the main issues, definitions and practical advice that have proven to be helpful to individuals, families and counsellors since I first started to work in the field in the late 1970s.

This publication will serve two main purposes. It will be a useful handbook for both the preventative education of an unsuspecting society, as well as offering guidance to those with a loved one or professional colleague currently enmeshed in a cult. People need facts and clear direction as quickly as possible. Wading through the many excellent but lengthy books on the subject is likely to be a more attractive prospect once the basics, found in this booklet, are understood.

It can be used as a teaching tool, especially by institutions that do not have the time or funds for a public speaker on the topic. It can also be used as a resource by people in the caring professions and the corporate world.

Additional leaflets and other information for educational institutions, the religious community and corporations can be obtained by contacting the Cult Information Centre as shown below:

Cult Information Centre,
BCM CULTS, London, WC1N 3XX
Tel: 0845 4500 868
Website: www.cultinformation.org.uk

Profits generated from the sale of this booklet will go to the Cult Information Centre, a registered charity.

Foreword

As Founder of the Samaritans (1953) and of Befrienders International (1974), I encountered every depressing situation which could lead to despair and even suicide. It wasn't long before the devastating effects of the activities of cults had to be added to other horrors, and ignorance about their nature and methods was almost universal. Since 1977 the deaths they have caused have been widely reported in the media, and since 1993 hardly a year has passed without its newsworthy horror.

Anyone touched by this insidious phenomenon needs information and guidance, and I know of no more reliable book than *Cults: A practical guide* by Ian Haworth. I am proud to have been a Patron since the Cult Information Centre started.

Chad Varah.

Prebendary Dr Chad Varah, CH, CBE, MA, DSc.
1911-2007

Chapter 1

Exploding the myths

"An ounce of prevention is worth a pound of cure."

Why we need this booklet

Cults. For most of us, our only contact with them is the occasional brush in the street with a member, or else a tragedy reported on the news. Most people assume that the problem is small, isolated, and on the decrease. Contrary to what many imagine, however, cults are alive and well in the UK and on the increase: and both the membership and numbers of cult groups are growing. It is safe to say that there are well over 500 different cults operating in the UK today.

At least one of these groups has over 700 different corporate names, which some people describe as 'front names'. Consequently, this makes the problem of discernment a major one.

Unless people understand the methodology of a typical cult, it is only too easy to be drawn into their sphere of influence. In addition, if counsellors, educators and others in positions of responsibility in the UK are not aware of what constitutes a cult and how cults operate, then they will be ill-equipped to help people confronted by cult-related issues.

The purpose of the booklet is to provide an easy-to-read, condensed overview of the key issues surrounding cults. It will focus on giving sound, practical help to those personally affected by cults, as well as to those who wish to get a clearer picture, for research purposes, of how cults operate.

Who is it for?

The booklet is written for a wide variety of readers, as follows:

★ For students and staff in schools:
- to warn them of the dangers of cults.
- to assist them in their research into the general cult phenomenon.

★ For families and friends of cult members to enable them to understand quickly the basics of cultism to:
- help them avoid making unnecessary mistakes in their communications with the cult member.
- help them to take the initiative in trying to neutralise the influence of the cult.

★ For families and friends of ex-cult members to help them understand:
- what they are likely to encounter in their own emotions.
- what the ex-cult member will be expe-

riencing so that they can better assist in his/her recovery.

★ For ex-cult members to help them understand what has happened to them and to understand and accelerate the recovery period.

★ For counsellors, clergy, medical and mental health professionals to assist them in understanding the sometimes complex issues surrounding cult involvement so they are better equipped to:
  • warn those with whom they are in touch.
  • offer better help to grieving families that have lost a loved one to a cult.
  • offer better support for ex-cult members experiencing withdrawal after leaving a cult.

★ For executives and personnel managers in the corporate world to assist in warning their staff or in helping those already damaged by cults.

WARNING !

With the best of intentions, some people try to infiltrate a cult in order to learn more about it for academic or other personal reasons. **WE DO NOT RECOMMEND THIS COURSE OF ACTION.**

Nobody is immune to the influence of the mind-control techniques used by cults. These techniques of psychological coercion can work, whether or not an individual is forewarned of the use of such methods. Since cult mind-control practices result in an impairment of one's ability to think and crit-

ically evaluate, the last person to recognise that harm is being done to him or her is the victim.

It is with this in mind that we give this warning and in the interests of public health and safety. Hopefully, if this warning is not fully appreciated by the reader at this stage, it will be, once you have read what follows.

Exploding the myths

In this booklet we have tried to suggest that cults represent a serious threat to the mental health and welfare of the individual and the family. Unfortunately, in Britain there is a great deal of confusion and misinformation surrounding this issue and myths abound. Many of these myths are the result of cult propaganda. Some are a result of the work of pro-cult activists. Others exist merely because the average person prefers to be in denial and say, 'It could never happen to me.'

It is hoped that by reading this booklet most of the myths surrounding the cult issue will be exploded. We would like to underline the following:

1. People don't join cults. They are recruited.

2. People are recruited by a method, not a message.

3. People do not stay in cults because they have nothing better to do with their lives, but because psychological coercion holds them there.

4. Cults intend to retain a hold on people for life, or for as long as they are valuable to the cult. It is not a fad or a phase.

5. Normal people from normal families are recruited into cults.

6. Cults should be blamed for the problems

caused, not the individual members, ex-members or their families (blame the victim syndrome). **It can happen to anyone.**

7. Cult members are sincere. (Sincere victims, but sincere.)

8. Cult members are victims and need to be treated with love. They are people who need help, not hostility.

9. Cults recruit people of all ages. Not just young people.

10. Cult recruiters are rarely visually identifiable. They usually look like quite normal people who appear to be very friendly.

11. Anyone can become a victim of cult techniques of psychological coercion. However, the safest people are those who know how to recognise a cult.

12 Accurate information on cults is not best obtained by trying to infiltrate a cult. **This is far too dangerous.**

Chapter 2

A brief history of Cults

"Injustice anywhere is a threat to justice everywhere. "

Martin Luther King Jr

There have clearly been periods in history when a variety of new groups with new philosophies have arisen. These groups may have been spin-offs from mainline religions or quite individual and independent of any other worldview. However, these groups can be best described as sects and were quite different from what are described as cults (see definition in chapter 3) today.

Cults are essentially a post-war phenomenon. Most cults have arisen since the late 1960s and new groups are continually being formed. Initially most people recognised cults as 'religious', which did and still do form the majority of cults in contemporary society. However, the other main category of cults, 'therapy cults', have flourished since the early 1970s and continue to do so today. These cults do not present themselves as religious in any way, but rather as a whole variety of 'personal improvement' organisations. Their essence, however, remains the same.

Society responded, and from the late 1970s onwards, small grassroots 'counter-cult' organisations formed around the world. They monitored cult activity, counselled families that had lost loved ones to cults, and exposed the damaging and deceptive recruitment techniques employed by cults.

The importance of the work of the earliest counter-cult groups was underlined by the 'Jonestown' tragedy on 18th November 1978, when 913 members of the People's Temple group died in Guyana after obeying the order of their cult leader, Jim Jones, to drink Kool-Aid grape juice laced with cyanide. That one event probably did more to highlight the dangers of cults and help cult critics than any other.

The cults quickly responded to the growing number of counter-cult groups by trying to smear and intimidate their critics. Many cults vigorously attack through the law courts anyone who attempts to expose them. This is one of the reasons why we have avoided mentioning specific contemporary cults in this booklet.

The 1970s also saw the emergence of small 'counter counter-cult' organisations mainly comprising a handful of pro-cult academics who were encouraged and sometimes financially aided by the cults. These groups have tried to muddy the water and suggest, with differing degrees of success, that cults were relatively harmless.

However, more and more people joined the ranks of the cult critics, including some scholars in the scientific community. They recognised the methods of cults and compared them with brainwashing techniques previously used against prisoners of war in Indo-China and Korea. Terms like 'psychological coercion', 'thought reform' and 'mind control' were being used to describe typical cult methods of recruitment.

Some were seeing the work of psychologist Dr William Sargant, in his books *Battle for the Mind* and *The Mind Possessed,* in a new and even more relevant light. The work of Dr Robert Lifton in his book *Thought Reform and the Psychology of Totalism* soon became recognised as a classic work for aiding people to understand the methods and growth of cults. Academic papers and books written by Dr Margaret T. Singer (University of California), the late Dr John G. Clarke Jnr. (Harvard University), Dr Andrew Malcolm (Toronto), and the researchers Flo Conway and Jim Siegelman (New York) added further weight to increasing concerns about the destructive nature of cult methods.

As the war of information between the cults, the counter-cult groups and the counter counter-cult groups continued, the cults grew, but perhaps less quickly than would have been the case if unchallenged. Along with the growth in numbers and membership of cults came the inevitable growth in income of the individual cults.

As the years passed some cults took the opportunity to start business enterprises. The pool of ready and willing cult members who would work long hours for little reward made the organisations very wealthy. With a large investment of accumulated cash, they were able to diversify and operate far fewer labour-intensive financial concerns than had originally been the case. Most of the money in the early days had been generated by deceptive begging on city streets.

Cults also operated in the business world on another front. By the late 1980s the therapy cults had recruited sufficient numbers of professional people to have begun to have some influence in a few large corporations. By the late 1990s the problem seemed to be increasing at an alarming rate, so much so that cults seem likely to pose a significant and increasing threat to employees in the corporate world in the early 21st century.

Cult tragedies in recent history

1969: Manson Family—Actress Sharon Tate and her guests killed by followers of Charles Manson

1974: Symbionese Liberation Army, USA - (Recruited Patty Hearst). Members died after siege and fire

1978: People's Temple—Jonestown, Guyana - 18th November (913 died)

1984: The Move - Philadelphia, USA—1984 (Members died after siege and fire)

1993: Branch Davidians - Waco, Texas, USA—April 1993 (83 Members died after siege and fire)

1994: Solar Temple-Switzerland & Canada—September (53 died)

1995: Aum Shinrikyo—Japan—March (Over 5,000 injured, 16 died)

1995: Solar Temple—France—December (16 died)

1997: Solar Temple—Canada—March (5 died)

1997: Heaven's Gate—California—March (39 died)

2000: The Restoration of the Ten Commandments of God - Uganda (1,000+ believed to have died)

Chapter 3

Understanding the issues

"People are enticed by a message but controlled by a method."

The extent of the problem

It is conservatively estimated that there are well over 500 cults that are currently active in the UK. This means that on a *per capita* basis, the UK has a similar problem to that facing people in the USA, where there are five times as many cults and five times as many people.

Many cults referred to as 'religious cults' register as religious institutions and are able to realise the tax benefits associated with that status. In addition, when they are criticised for inappropriate behaviour, they often suggest they are being persecuted. They seem to use the laws of religious liberty in the UK as a licence to do anything in the name of a faith.

Other cults register as non-religious institutions and tend to offer very intensive courses, often over a long weekend, claiming to assist people via a new therapy or self-help programme. These cults are described as 'therapy cults'.

The majority of cults fit into one of the categories described above. However, it is not illegal to form a cult, and vast sums of money can be generated for their leaders. The wealth they soon generate allows them to initiate lawsuits against their critics for alleged libel or slander.

Whether or not a case has merit, unless the defendant fights the case at great cost, the case will be lost. Few people have the resources to oppose such an action, which can bankrupt the defendants and 'gag' them in the process. As a consequence, freedom to speak about the cults is severely limited and less information than is appropriate is available to an unsuspecting public.

With the above in mind, it is perhaps not surprising that cults in the UK are flourishing. They are recruiting from the religious and non-religious community, the corporate world, educational institutions, clubs, societies and from within the family.

The main concern about cult activity, from the author's perspective, is that of the psychologically coercive methods that cults, by definition, use to recruit. However, **it is not illegal to use these methods** and thus there is no protection for society, except by educating people so that they are equipped with the tools that help people to determine what may be a cult, prior to their becoming involved with it. It is my hope that this booklet will be a part of that educational process.

DEFINITION OF A CULT:

Every cult can be defined as a group having all of the following five characteristics:

1. It uses psychological coercion to recruit, indoctrinate and retain its members.
2. It forms an elitist totalitarian society.
3. Its founder-leader is self-appointed, dogmatic, messianic, not accountable and has charisma.
4. It believes 'the end justifies the means' in order to solicit funds or recruit people. (Called 'heavenly deception' in one group).
5. Its wealth does not benefit its members or society.

Certain groups may exhibit some or many of these characteristics, but you should not assume that a group is a cult just because it exhibits one or two of the above features.

CATEGORIES OF CULT

RELIGIOUS CULTS
Communal living is common.

Members usually do not join the general workforce.

Average age at the point of recruitment is in the low 20s.

Registered as religious groups.

Appear to offer association with a group making the world a better place via political, spiritual or other means.

THERAPY CULTS
Communal living is rare.

Members keep their ordinary job.

Average age at the point of recruitment is in the mid 30s.

Registered as 'non profit making'.

Appear to offer association with a group giving courses in some kind of therapy or self-improvement technique.

The above list of cult category characteristics is a generalisation and we understand that there may be exceptions to some of the points.

Cult mind-control techniques

Control over the mind of a potential cult recruit can easily be achieved in the average cult in a matter of 3 or 4 days. This is achieved by using a combination of mind-control techniques against the unsuspecting individual. These techniques, which are listed below, break people down physically and mentally, and remove their ability to think freely and critically for themselves.

Who do they recruit?

Too often rational people say, "It could never happen to me. I could never be recruited into a cult." They wrongly assume and often suggest about cult members that before they were recruited...

- they were inadequate people
- they were obviously people without direction in their lives
- they were probably not very intelligent
- they must come from dysfunctional families
- they must have had no self esteem
- they were probably not well educated
- they probably had no faith
- they were lost souls, searching for something
- they were teenagers who had nothing better to do.

It seems that people want to believe there has to be a special something that makes a person 'vulnerable'. They do not realise that people do not 'join' cults, but are instead actively recruited. They have a reluctance to believe that it could happen to them or someone that they know. It is true that anyone can be recruited by a cult if they are not able to recognise the cult in advance and have the strength to walk away from it.

Nevertheless, there are some people who are more likely to be recruited. They are of any age and will usually have most of the following characteristics...

THE LIKELY RECRUIT:
1. Upper income family background.
2. Average to above average intelligence.
3. Good education.
4. Idealistic.

Except for the last item, most people would find this a surprising list, but the statistics show a clear pattern.

What harm do they do?

When the average person is recruited into a cult, they undergo a profound personality change. This occurs in most cases at that point when they succumb to the techniques of mind control. At the same time, cult members lose much of their ability to critically evaluate what is happening to them.

The person has become an unwitting member of a psychologically coercive organisation, but is programmed to say and feel that the cult is marvellous, that they are there of their own free will and that the group is *definitely* not a cult. The new cult member will now do whatever they are programmed to do, whether or not it is...

- against their former moral code
- against their former religious beliefs
- against their family's best interests
- against their own financial interests
- against their own physical and mental well-being
- against their employer's accepted code of practice

- against the interests of society
- against the law.

In the above mindset, one can see that the cult member is now at serious risk not just from the psychological pressures that have been brought to bear, but also from carrying out whatever instructions the cult leader might give.

Harm comes to the family too. They have seen the problems for themselves and often been faced with hostility when trying to intervene. The heartbreak they suffer is difficult to compare with anything else. In one family one child had died and the other had been recruited into a cult. The parents said that the recruitment of their son into a cult was harder for them to deal with. "It was a living death. There was nothing final, such as a burial. It was like trying to cope with a sort of living death." Their pain, their heartache and their grief went on and on and on.

The grievous harm that cults do to people and families is most obvious when we see the headlines about mass deaths. This however, is just the tip of the iceberg. Cult members too often find themselves facing psychiatric breakdowns because of their involvement. Some members fall ill or become physically injured because of the cult regime. Cults are

Mind-control techniques

HYPNOSIS Inducing a state of high suggestibility by hypnosis, often thinly disguised as relaxation or meditation.

PEER GROUP PRESSURE Suppressing doubt and resistance to new ideas by exploiting the need to belong.

LOVE BOMBING Creating a sense of family and belonging through hugging, kissing, touching and flattery.

REJECTION OF OLD VALUES Accelerating acceptance of new lifestyle by constantly denouncing former values and beliefs.

CONFUSING DOCTRINE Encouraging blind acceptance and rejection of logic through complex lectures on an incomprehensible doctrine.

METACOMMUNICATION Implanting subliminal messages by stressing certain key words or phrases in long, confusing lectures.

REMOVAL OF PRIVACY Achieving loss of ability to evaluate logically by preventing private contemplation.

TIME SENSE DEPRIVATION Destroying ability to evaluate information, personal reactions, and body functions in relation to passage of time by removing all clocks and watches.

DISINHIBITION Encouraging child-like obedience by orchestrating child-like behaviour.

UNCOMPROMISING RULES Inducing regression and disorientation by soliciting agreement to seemingly simple rules which regulate mealtimes, bathroom breaks and use of medications.

VERBAL ABUSE Desensitizing through bombardment with foul and abusive language.

SLEEP DEPRIVATION AND FATIGUE Creating disorientation and vulnerability by prolonging mental and physical activity and withholding adequate rest and sleep.

DRESS CODES Removing individuality by

rarely caring towards those who crack under the pressure. Instead, these people are often simply pushed out to fend for themselves.

Even those cult members able to escape from the cult usually suffer from symptoms of withdrawal for a year or more. This destructive harvest rarely makes the headlines, but leaves many thousands of people blighted every year, often for life. Families and society as a whole are left to pick up the pieces and pay the financial and emotional bills.

Why do they do it?

Whatever a cult may claim to be motivated by, it is inevitable that two common denominators are found. They are the control of people using psychological coercion and the amassing of wealth. With money and people a cult leader has power.

The quest for power is surely a key motivator for many cult leaders. This power over others may be used to try to implement plans of a political nature. It may be used to sexually exploit the members of the cult. It may simply be used to satisfy the leader's inadequacies and their lust for power.

Perhaps some cult leaders are simply motivated by greed and are ruthlessly focused on acquiring as much wealth as possible at the

---

demanding conformity to the group dress code.

CHANTING AND SINGING Eliminating non-cult ideas through group repetition of mind-narrowing chants or phrases.

CONFESSION Encouraging the destruction of individual ego through confession of personal weaknesses and innermost feelings or doubts.

FINANCIAL COMMITMENT Achieving increased dependence on the group by 'burning bridges' to the past, through the donation of assets.

FINGER POINTING Creating a false sense of righteousness by pointing to the shortcomings of the outside world and other cults.

FLAUNTING HIERARCHY Promoting acceptance of cult authority by promising advancement, power and salvation.

ISOLATION Inducing loss of reality by physical separation from family, friends, society and rational references.

CONTROLLED APPROVAL Maintaining vulnerability and confusion by alternately rewarding and punishing similar actions.

CHANGE OF DIET Creating disorientation and increased susceptibility to emotional arousal by depriving the nervous system of necessary nutrients through the use of special diets and/or fasting.

GAMES Inducing dependence on the group by introducing games with obscure rules.

NO QUESTIONS Accomplishing automatic acceptance of beliefs by discouraging questions.

GUILT Reinforcing the need for 'salvation' by exaggerating the sins of the former lifestyles.

FEAR Maintaining loyalty and obedience to the group by threatening soul, life or limb for the slightest 'negative' thought, word or deed.

REPLACEMENT OF RELATIONSHIPS Destroying pre-cult families by arranging cult marriages and 'families'.

expense of innocent lives.

Some cult leaders may have started their movement with good intentions, but, as the saying goes, 'the power of love has become the love of power'. Before long one finds that 'power corrupts and absolute power corrupts absolutely'.

Other cult leaders may be initially motivated by personal financial gain but, after a number of months or years start to believe their own propaganda.

There are of course some cult leaders who have delusions of grandeur and believe that they are prophets or gods or have some other unique ability and/or insight into the future. These cult leaders are probably the ones that are more likely to provoke future acts of violence against their membership and others in society. Their mental health may well be questioned and found lacking. This makes

The difference between religions and cults

This is not an exhaustive list, and note that some religions, churches or groups that are, by and large, legitimate, can sometimes display some cult-like characteristics. Similarly, cults will try to use the language of genuine religion, and present themselves as legitimate.

Religion	Cult
Conversion	Coercion
Commitment freely chosen	Commitment via psychological force
Between individual and God	Between individual and group
Empowers members	Disempowers members
Increases discernment	Decreases discernment
Unconditional love for members	Conditional love for members
Recognises and values the family	Alienates members from family
Growth and maturing of members	Regression and stunting of members
Individual uniqueness	Cloned personalities
Happiness and fulfilment	Artificial 'high'
Unity	Uniformity
Truth leads to experience	Experience becomes 'Truth'
Accountability of leadership	No accountability of leadership
Questioning encouraged	Questioning discouraged
Honesty prevails	The end justifies the means
Does not hide behind fronts	Hides behind fronts

the likelihood of a paranoid reaction against their members and society a more likely prospect than with cult leaders that are, for example, financially motivated.

So what's the difference?

Some people, particularly those outside of the religious community, have difficulty differentiating between a religious cult and a legitimate religious institution. On the surface, there are similarities, but in reality there are major differences. The differences are listed in the table on page 16.

Therapy or cult?

Others in society wonder if the so called 'therapy cults' are vastly different to legitimate therapy sessions one might have with a recognised professional therapist. There seem to be many differences, including those listed in the table below.

The difference between therapies and cults

Again, this is not an exhaustive list. Some self-help groups, and indeed, clinical psychology can use some of the control techniques described, but it is the whole package and the motivation behind it that determines the essential difference.

Therapy	Cult
Rehabilitates	Debilitates
Objective: goals agreed by client	Objective: leader's goals
Promotes healthy relationships with others	Fosters alienation from others
Aim: independence of client	Aim: dependence of member
Psychologically enables the client	Psychologically disables the members
Questioning encouraged	Questioning discouraged
Decision-making ability enhanced	Decision-making ability impaired
Therapist accountable	Cult leader not accountable
Qualifications recognised by outside body	Self appointed
Fees agreed in advance	Fees often inflated once member is under mind control
For benefit of client	For benefit of leader
Does not hide behind fronts	Hides behind fronts

Just like the army?

Some people, who perhaps have not understood the power of mind control techniques in a typical cult, assume that life in a cult may be similar to that of life in the army. They are mistaken for many reasons, some of which are outlined below.

The difference between military service and cults

Army	Cult
No deception to lure potential recruits or to lure the unsuspecting into group	Deception and false love (love-bombing)
Outside contact allowed and promoted	Outside contact often controlled and alienation from outsiders promoted
True motives shown ahead of time	True motives hidden
Appropriate information and time given before taking first step	Misinformation and little time given before commitment
Informed choice	Non-informed psychological coercion
Join for previously agreed period	Recruited unknowingly for life
New recruits spend time together and support each other	New recruits separated from each other to help break down support systems
Education	Indoctrination
Build you up physically	Often break you down physically
Adequate sleep and rest given	Sleep deprivation routinely used
Adequate food and balanced diet	Often inadequate food, sometimes low in protein and high in carbohydrates
Medical problems taken care of	Medical problems often disregarded
Family respected and cherished	Family often ridiculed and alienated
Free when off duty	Often monitored when away from group
Caters for different spiritual perspectives	One worldview indoctrinated into members
Members remunerated for their services	Members exploited financially
Serving interests of the democratic state	Serving interests of leader
Can choose to leave of own free will at end of contract	Can leave only if and when psychological hold is first broken

Getting to Know the 'Master'
A Diary of Cult Recruitment

This fictional account shows some of the characteristics and techniques of cult recruitment in action

20th April
This new job is great—I've hardly had time to catch my breath! It is really exciting, I just hope I can keep up with the pace. I need more energy from somewhere and the double cappuccinos just aren't doing the trick! Trouble is, I'm getting home and my mind is still racing with ideas. Tom being away on business doesn't help. Only the cat to offload to. Had an interesting chat to Liz from the advertising department today, though. I was letting off steam about this new deadline and she started telling me about this class she goes along to that does some sort of relaxation therapy. Said it would give me lots more positive energy. Wants me to go along with her to an 'open evening' they are running tomorrow. Not really my cup of tea, but she had been so sweet listening to me ramble on about work that I didn't like to say no. I'd already told her that I wasn't doing anything that night too. Still, might be a bit of fun and you never know, it might help.

22nd April
What a strange evening! I thought it was just some sort of class, but it turns out that it is a bit more than that. They meet every week and run these weekend courses and retreats. Most of the people at the Centre seem to be regulars and they seem to all be very close. At first I felt a bit odd. I thought is this some sort of weird cult or what? But then this really nice guy came

up and started chatting to me and introduced me to some of the others. Liz had told them I was coming and they seemed so pleased to see me. They made me feel really welcome. Lots of interesting people—lawyers, a doctor and quite a few media types—really intelligent, so it must be okay. Don't remember much of the lecture, deadly dull and a bit over my head. I asked some questions afterwards but Liz said that if I really wanted to find out more why not come along to a weekend retreat. I told her my weekends were pretty tied up with Tom and everything and she seemed really disappointed.

The relaxation bit was good. I felt really calm and sort of 'spaced out' afterwards and the strange thing was that I thought it had only been about five minutes, but it was actually more like half an hour. I had no sense of time at all! Afterwards, though, I overheard some guy talking about 'The Master' and so I said to Liz 'Oh who is he? Is he like your guru or something?' and she got really flustered. Alexander who gave the talk must have overheard because he came up and explained that it was just an Eastern thing, you know, an honorary title given to the man who developed the exercises. Not a guru at all.

I got the distinct impression I had said something I shouldn't. Felt a bit reticent about asking any more questions after that.

25th April
Another hair-raising day with these deadlines. Tried to do the breathing exercise I learnt the other night, but it didn't help much. Maybe I need a copy of the tape of chanting that they used. They had it playing in the background. I asked Liz about it

and she said that sometimes you need to have the support of the group to really get the hang of it. She mentioned the retreat again and I said I would think about it. Not really keen—but she has been so nice to me. She said how everyone at the group thought I was great and that my questions were really perceptive. That made me feel really good about myself.

4th May

Tom was back this morning and surprise, surprise, we had a flaming argument! There was I wanting to spend a quiet, romantic weekend with him and he's got to work. He's booked a squash game with one of his mates from work too! He said never mind, we can spend next weekend together down at his parents'. Not exactly romantic—so I said I had made plans too and told him about the retreat. He was furious! Didn't I know how much his parents were looking forward to seeing us, how could I think of spending that much money when we were saving so hard, on and on. In the end I said I wouldn't go.

5th May

Last night Peter from the Centre rang me to ask if I was going on the retreat. He was so understanding and sweet. He asked me if Tom always tried to control me like that and was he always so negative. Hadn't really thought about it like that, but I thought well, yes, he is. Peter said this retreat would really help me relax more and clarify what I wanted out of life. After all, he said, if I didn't know what my needs were how would I know if they were being met?

So I thought, *why not?* I deserve it. I've been working really hard and I deserve a break. Peter said he could just squeeze me in so I gave him my credit card details and signed up there and then. Liz phoned me about 20 minutes afterwards, really thrilled. I felt so pleased about it.

13th May

What an amazing weekend! It was so good to get away from the flat. Tom had been really sour about me going, making sarcastic comments all week. I chatted with Peter about it because I almost felt like pulling out again. He is so understanding. He asked if Tom might consider coming along to an open evening. No way, I said, he thinks it's all a load of nonsense. Then Peter said that if this was the case, it was probably best if I didn't really talk about it with Tom. If all he was going to do was be negative, then it would just drain my life energy away. He said he could tell from the start that I had a really high level of spiritual energy and that would make me very sensitive to negative vibrations. He emailed me a questionnaire to fill out before I went—sort of an inventory of the high points and low points throughout my life, why I wanted to do the retreat etc, etc.

Anyway I eventually made it to the weekend. The group has this fantastic old house in the middle of the countryside that was given to them by one of their members, a businessman, who reckoned that the Master's teachings had saved his life. Quite a few of the members live there, training to be teachers of the techniques themselves. They were great, really focused and with a real sense of purpose to make the world a better place. Made me think—what am I doing?

We spent lots of time doing the techniques and 'centring' ourselves as they call it. I was welcomed with open arms. Everyone seemed so pleased to see me, they made me feel so special. I felt quite emotional. We had a time of sharing after one of the sessions. I feel so close to these people. They seem to really know and understand me. Then on the Sunday there was a question and answer session with a woman from the USA. Apparently she is the Master's right hand, so to speak.

People were asking her questions about what they should be doing, even in one case whether they should leave their partner! It all seemed a bit heavy and I felt quite uncomfortable, but then she looked at me and smiled and told me all this stuff about myself that she couldn't possibly have known, about my childhood and work and Tom. You know, stuff about not feeling appreciated or supported, feeling inadequate and misunderstood. I guess I do feel these things. I just burst into tears and they all hugged me. It was wonderful. Later Liz told me what an honour it was for someone new to be singled out like that, because this woman is apparently really spiritual.

Then before I drove back Alexander, who runs the house, gave us a talk about the Master. He was the guy who spoke at the open meeting. How I could have ever thought it dull I really don't know. It was fascinating. The Master sounds amazing. He was this really successful businessman but then he had sort of a near death experience and a powerful spiritual encounter. His whole being became saturated with what they call the 'Divine Essence' and he has devoted his whole life ever since to teaching people techniques for discovering who they really are. Relaxation is just the tip of the iceberg. Alexander says we all have this spiritual destiny, a path to follow and until we find it and follow it, we will never be truly happy or fulfilled.

The Master's aim in life is to help people find this path. He's given his whole life to the service of mankind, even though it has meant he had to leave his wife and family to do so. They were all really encouraging me to come along to the weekly session that the group is doing at the Centre so that I could find out more and even watch the Master on video. I left on a real high! I can't remember when I have felt so good.

20th May
An awful week. Tom and I argued again (about the group of course). He is really threatened by my going along. He says I seem to be at the Centre or on the phone to them all the time. He just doesn't want me to grow and find myself. I felt so tired after the weekend. I guess I am not used to getting up at the crack of dawn for a class—especially after being up until nearly midnight the night before. I have been trying the diet that Alexander recommended to cleanse my body of toxins, but I really miss the chocolate! The Master says, apparently, that if you are connected to the Divine Essence your body doesn't need as much food. I noticed that the residents at the house hardly ate a thing! Its amazing how they can do that.

23rd May
Midweek I felt really quite depressed. I just couldn't seem to focus on work. Maybe I am in the wrong job? It all seems so pointless. Felt better after going to the Centre though. Peter asked me if I could think of anyone else who might benefit from the techniques. He said it was selfish of us to keep the benefits all to ourselves. I said that Tom's nephew was coming to stay for a few days and that he might be interested. He's a student in his second year and, like most guys of his age, a bit sceptical, but I know his course is really pressured and he has just broken up with his girl-friend.

Peter seemed really pleased with this and suggested that I stress to him how the techniques would help him with his studies, but not to mention about the Divine Essence or the Master, because he wouldn't really understand all that and why should that be a barrier to him getting help. He is so sensitive and caring.

13th June
The last few weeks have been awesome.

My life has changed so much I can hardly believe it. Tom and I had a huge row when he found out that I had encouraged his nephew along to the group. They put him in touch with some people near his hall of residence who do the techniques and he is even going on to a retreat in a couple of weeks. Tom's wholly negative and energy-depleting reaction made me really stop and take stock. I went to the Centre and talked it over with Peter and some of the others.

They really helped me realise just how dangerous it was to my spiritual well-being to stay with Tom. He is just draining the Divine Essence out of me. At first I was really sad. I mean, I do love him and we have been so happy together but the group helped me to see that we each have a spiritual destiny to follow and mine is taking me on a different path to his. It would be wrong of me to expect someone who was not spiritually awakened to understand this. It will be the best thing for him too in the long run and one day he will realise this.

15th June

Today Liz told me that Catharine, the woman from the USA who spoke at the retreat, had spoken to the Master about me. About me! He had said that when he comes to England next month he would give me personal instruction in the techniques and something called 'energy clearance', which is like this amazing experience. I can't wait. On top of this Alexander has said that I can come and stay at the house where we had the retreat, for as long as I like. That is so great—otherwise I would have to stay in the flat with Tom until we sell it and can both find somewhere else to live. I don't think I could stand that, but now I will be living with people who really care about me and with whom I share a common goal. Wow, that's so positive! To begin with I thought—what about work? But then Peter helped me to see that my spiritual destiny was more important than mere material things. He is so right. And besides, he says that the group could really use someone with my skills to work on their magazine, so there will be plenty for me to do.

16th June

My boss was really shocked when I told her I was handing in my notice. She said that I had not seemed like my old self for a few months, sort of distant and not quite there, and that she had been worried that I was having some sort of breakdown. For a second it made me think, hang on a minute, am I doing the right thing and I started to get a bit panicky. But then I remembered the exercise I had been taught to do when faced with unexpected negativity. I just tuned her out and soon felt much better! How blind these people are!

The Master is right—the un-awakened can really destroy your sense of spiritual balance. Best to have as little to do with them as possible...

Chapter 4

How to help cult members

"When it comes to cults, it's all in the mind."

Changes to expect in a typical cult recruit

One of the most frightening things for friends and family is the way that people change when they are recruited into a cult. These changes are immediate and obvious. Rarely, however, do people recognise them for what they are, or consider the possibility that it is caused by cult involvement. The following are some of the changes that are typical in a cult recruit:

- Sudden drastic personality change— 'Snapping'
- Aggressively defensive
- Appears distant – trance state common – detached
- Change of expression
- Withdrawn and secretive
- Loss of abstractions and metaphors
- New language – cult jargon
- Reduced capacity to form flexible and intimate relationships
- New diet
- Appears cold or emotionless to former family and friends
- New social group

- Physical deterioration–lost sleep, inadequate diet, overworked
- Loss of sense of humour
- Neurotic, psychotic or suicidal tendencies
- Loss of critical ability – judgement impaired
- Interest in new literature
- Hypersensitive to criticism
- Inappropriately effervescent.

Please note again that, on its own, the appearance of one of these characteristics (with the possible exception of 'snapping') does not prove cult involvement. It is the broader picture, involving several of the features at once, that should arouse suspicions that all is not right.

Understanding cult members

When one considers what has been done psychologically to cult members, as outlined in the last chapter, then one can perhaps appreciate that there are going to be difficulties in communicating effectively with them.

Cult members have undergone a profound change. Although family and friends see and know this to be a change for the worse, cult victims are programmed to feel good about the change, and to equate the change with 'conversion' or 'enlightenment' or 'getting in touch with ultimate reality'. They are no longer able to critically evaluate to the degree that was possible prior to recruitment into the cult. Simple issues that appear to be obvious to the average person, who is still able to think clearly, are difficult to understand for cult members.

As a consequence, when family and friends try lovingly and desperately to point out the obvious to cult members, they are met with vacant expressions often followed by programmed smug looks of superiority.

What is true, moral or legal to cult members is now what they are programmed to understand, which needs no basis in reality at all. Many cult members are programmed to lie and to misrepresent the nature and/or identity of the cult. The end justifies the means. Because cult members do so as a programmed response, it is automatic and done with apparent sincerity. Indeed cult members are sincere. However, they are sincerely wrong and sincerely misguided. They are sincere victims.

It is important to understand this mindset of cult members, otherwise communication will tend to quickly become more and more heated and frustrating for all concerned. Eventually, the result of continuing to engage in ineffective dialogue will be that feelings will tend to boil over and turn into expressions of anger, which in turn will often result in a breakdown of communication.

It is with this in mind that the list of 'Dos and Don'ts' on the opposite page is offered as a guideline. Following it should help most families and friends of cult members to avoid most of the pitfalls and maintain some kind of contact with the cult recruit.

Dealing with families

For every person who is recruited into a cult there are usually at least three other people left on the 'sidelines' grieving for that loved one and needing help and direction. They are the family.

When a family loses someone to a cult, it is an experience they will never forget and one they would prefer not to be repeated. The loving family member of yesterday has undergone a dramatic change of personality. The family are now trying to communicate with a stranger, who seems to be a physical clone of the person they knew, but with the wiring changed. It is a shocking and frightening experience for the average family or friend of a cult member. As has already been discussed in Chapter 3, losing a loved one to a cult has been equated with the suffering associated with bereavement.

When the family tries to get help, they are usually met with disbelief or simply complete ignorance. Some people, with the best intentions, are likely to suggest it is "just a fad or a phase". Others will say, "It can't be a cult. Your husband is too intelligent to fall for that nonsense".

Those in the religious community will sometimes say, "We will pray about it," and do nothing more, instead expecting God to intervene to solve the problem, without any direct effort on their part.

The family soon feels very lost and lonely. Self doubt starts to creep in. They begin to

DOS AND DON'TS: Talking to and dealing with cult members

The Dos

Do try to keep in regular contact via mail or telephone even if there is little response.

Do express sincere love for the cult member at every available opportunity.

Do keep a diary of comments, attitudes and events associated with his/her life in the cult.

Do always welcome back the cult member into the family home no matter what is said.

Do keep copies of all written correspondence from you and the cult member.

Do record all the names, addresses and phone numbers of people linked with the cult.

Do try to bite your tongue if the cult member makes unkind comments.

Do read all the recommended books relating to cults, mind control and the specific cult.

Do seek help from organisations specialising in counter-cult work.

The Don'ts

Do not rush into adopting a potential solution before carefully researching the cult problem.

Do not say, "You are in a cult, you are brainwashed".

Do not give money to the member of the group.

Do not give away original cult documents to anyone. Provide copies only.

Do not feel guilty. This is not a problem caused by families.

Do not act in an angry or hostile manner towards the cult member.

Do not feel alone. It happens to thousands of families every year.

Do not underestimate the control the cult has over each member.

Do not antagonise the cult member by ridiculing his/her 'beliefs'.

Do not be judgmental or confrontational towards the cult member.

Do not antagonise any of the cult's leadership or other members.

Do not be persuaded to hire a cult 'specialist' without verifying his/her qualifications.

Do not give up hope of success, no matter how long it takes.

Do not neglect yourself or other family members.

wonder, "Are we overreacting after all? Perhaps it is not as bad as we first suspected. Surely if the group was as bad as we first thought, it would not be allowed to operate in this country." It becomes easier, in the face of such ignorance of the problem in society, to believe that it is they who are wrong and not the cult.

When family members are finally introduced to people who do understand the problem of cults, they have experienced an emotional rollercoaster ride and are often very upset, confused and exhausted.

Consequently, one should not underestimate the damage done to family members experiencing the loss of a loved one to a cult. They need clear direction, support and understanding in order to begin to effectively tackle the problem. By understanding the issues facing a family, one is better able to comfort, support and guide them. The following are some of the other situations, feelings and stresses they are likely to face:

- Parents of a cult member tend to feel guilty. There is sometimes self blame and the inevitable question for many families, "Where did we go wrong?" even though there need be no basis in reality for such a question.

- Children of a cult member may similarly blame themselves for not having helped to check the reliability of the group, before the parent went to that first meeting or course. They may dwell on the 'if only'.

- Fathers of cult members often have particular difficulty understanding and then coping with a loved one in a cult. I have talked with many families where the father has felt that it has been almost too difficult to bear. One father said, "It's just like being on a plane with no pilot and I haven't had flying lessons. I feel so helpless". Some fathers have had heart attacks because of the strain. Others have developed alcohol-related problems.

- Families often suffer from a lack of understanding by relatives, friends, police, clergy, medical and mental health professionals and politicians. This increases the stress on the family and adds to the confusion, and can increase their feelings of guilt and/or anger.

- Some families believe information they have received from the cult or from cult apologists and have initially taken the wrong action. This can add to their stress, frustration and general suffering.

- The stress of having a child in a cult can also have an adverse impact on the marriage. If however, one of the parents is the cult member, there are usually major difficulties in the marriage too.

- There can be an adverse impact on siblings, because all the attention tends to be focused on the brother or sister who is the cult member.

- A family may experience financial difficulties because of all the costs associated with having a loved one in a cult. The cult member may have given a large sum of family money to the cult. The family may have to pay for reverse-charged phone calls from wherever the cult member is located. There may be legal costs associated with the cult involvement. Family members may take flights to visit the cult member. There could be the costs of hiring other professional services.

Legal recourse for the family

There seems to be no protection in law from groups that use mind-control techniques to recruit unsuspecting, innocent people. It is therefore not usually possible for a family to go to court to try to reverse what a cult has already done and to free someone from the cult.

However, in situations where a parent has been recruited into a cult, the cult member parent may already have or try to gain custody, through the courts, of children in the family. In situations such as these the non-cult member parent can, in the writer's experience, normally expect to win a court action with appropriate expert witnesses. Sadly ,there are again no guarantees.

Sometimes a cult member may be illegally living in a foreign country with the cult. Some families have managed to have the loved one deported in such circumstances. Once back in the home country they will be physically nearer to their family, which may assist the family in their efforts to help the cult member to leave. However, the danger with this course of action is that it may alienate the cult member even more if it is understood that the deportation was provoked by the family. Consequently, all the pros and cons must be weighed in advance.

In most situations, any legal recourse that may be available to the family and/or the ex-cult member will only be possible once the cult member has been freed from the cult. This is covered on p.41.

Helping cult members to leave

At the beginning of the 21st century it is all too easy to be recruited into a cult. However, to assist someone to leave is usually an extremely difficult job that comes with no guarantee of success.

It is possible that something a cult member sees or hears in the cult, that is not supposed to be revealed to the membership, could provoke positive change by reactivating the cult member's critical mind. When a cult member breaks free from a cult because of this, the person is usually described as a 'walkaway'. A walkaway, like any other ex-cult member, will still suffer the typical symptoms of withdrawal and need counselling, support and information.

However, one could wait for the rest of the cult member's life for a loved one to walk away from a cult and it may not happen. After all, it is important to remember that cult members are recruited into a cult for life, or until they cease to be of value to the cult, which may never occur.

With the above in mind, it is hardly surprising that most families want to be proactive in trying to reverse the damage done by the cult to that loved one. They want to take steps to try to reactivate the critical mind of the cult member. In order to try to achieve this objective, there are two main courses of action for families to consider. They are the 'DIY approach' and 'exit counselling'.

The DIY (do it yourself) approach

This course of action requires family and friends of a cult member to work together as a team. They need to read extensively about the phenomenon of cults in general, and where possible, read any articles or books about the specific group in question.

It will also be helpful for the family to speak to other families that have been successful in helping a loved one to leave a cult. Speaking to ex-members of the same cult is also highly advantageous. Contacts such as these can usually be obtained with the help of a reliable counter-cult organisation.

By doing their homework they will soon know far more about the philosophy and psychology of the cult than the cult member would ever know while still in the group. Armed with this information and any knowledge they may have gleaned about any corrupt or illegal practices associated with the cult, they can start to communicate with their loved one in a new way. If they gently begin to plant 'seeds of doubt' into conversations, while adhering to the 'Dos and Don'ts' list already discussed, they can hope that eventually one of the seeds will grow. A family could be successful in a week or two but might need to continue this process for years before success is achieved. Whatever happens, a family should never give up hope of success.

Exit counselling

Exit counselling involves hiring the services of a third party, an 'exit counsellor'. This is someone who has developed skills in being able to talk to cult members with their consent. An exit counsellor is often, but not always, an ex-cult member who has first-hand experience of the nightmare of being in the grip of a cult.

A typical exit counsellor will understand the language of cult members, the psychological techniques used to recruit and indoctrinate unsuspecting recruits, and any other questionable practices associated with a cult. By engaging in conversation with the cult member, the exit counsellor attempts to reactivate the critical mind of the cult member through the counselling. The goal is therefore the same as that attempted by the DIY approach, but it is more direct.

It is a more expensive route to consider than DIY, because it involves the cost of hiring the exit counsellor's services. Because of the financial considerations, it is not a course of action that every family can pursue. However, when it works, it can bring about a speedier solution for all concerned than the DIY approach.

Many families try the DIY approach first and use exit counselling as the last resort, when it appears to them that all else thus far has failed. Exit counsellors can be contacted through reliable counter-cult organisations.

Useful tips for counselling a cult member

In counselling a typical cult member, there are three key topics that should be considered for discussion, whether or not the counselling is by an exit counsellor or family members adopting the DIY approach. They are the following:

1. The philosophy of the cult.
2. The mind control methods of the cult.
3. The corrupt practices associated with the cult.

By entering into discussion on subjects related to these three topics, the hope is to raise an issue that the cult member is not programmed to deal with. This issue is one that would bring a doubt or question to the mind of the cult member. The exit counsellor or family member would then be able to encourage the cult member to discuss the subject in depth.

An experienced exit counsellor cannot know ahead of time what precise issue might provoke critical thought in a cult member, but will be able to recognise it when it comes along. Like a good exit counsellor, family members need to develop their skills in being able to detect when they are and when they are not getting through to the cult member.

In order to enter into meaningful dialogue with the cult member, the person counselling first needs to understand the language used by the cult member, and be fully aware of the definitions for the words. Terms like salvation, God, sin, brother, sister, family, parents, truth, evil, prophet, God-consciousness, ultimate reality, oneness, conversion, breakthrough, etc, may have completely different meanings and significance to the cult member than you would normally attach to them.

If the cult member's language is not fully understood, then the counsellor and the cult member may be having two separate but simultaneous conversations, which will achieve little or nothing. If the counsellor is not sure of the meaning of certain terms, then he can always ask the cult member to explain their meaning.

Because mind control impairs a person's ability to critically evaluate, the philosophy of the average cult does not need to be very sophisticated and often isn't. It is often full of contradictions and/or inconsistencies. By discussing the philosophy of the cult with the cult member, the aim would be to try to expose such a flaw in the concepts promoted by the cult and try to get the cult member to critically evaluate the information.

Similarly, where the counsellor is aware of the cult's methods of mind control, these too can be exposed. By analysing psychological manipulation, as it relates to the cult, the aim would be to show the cult member that coercion in a cult should not be confused with 'conversion' or whatever other expression the cult may use. However, the counsellor would be wise to keep in mind that even though the cult member has become a victim of coercion, he has still had a very powerful experience and that cannot be denied.

In discussing issues related to any corrupt practices of the group, the points where the practices are not in harmony with the philosophy would also offer fertile ground for potential thought-provoking dialogue. In addition, where the corrupt practices have involved breaking the law, the legal as well as moral implications of this might be discussed.

In order to gather information about the philosophy and mind-control methods of a cult, there are sometimes articles or even books that have been published about spe-cific cults and they of course are very useful. However, when these sources are not available, those intending to counsel a cult member can, through asking relevant questions, glean a basic understanding of the philosophy and practices from the cult member. It is therefore possible to counsel someone out of a cult without any prior knowledge of the group, but it is obviously more difficult to do so.

It is also important to remember that the cult member is a victim and needs to be treated with respect. Family and friends should therefore avoid ridiculing the cult or the cult member. Not only is this counter productive but it shows the same lack of respect for the individual for which cults themselves are notorious.

The aim for anyone doing the counselling is not to win the argument, or prove that you are right, but instead to help the cult member re-evaluate the group and his association with it. A common statement in the field of counselling cult victims is, "If I can get him to ask that first question, then I am probably on the road to success." The primary objective of any such counselling is therefore to reactivate the critical mind of the cult victim. This in turn gives back to the ex-member his free choice and the ability for self-determination.

Steven Hassan's books *Combatting Cult Mind Control*, (Park Street Press) and *Releasing The Bonds*, (Freedom of Mind Press) are particularly useful for families and counsellors of cult victims.

Chapter 5
Looking after ex-cult members

"Getting a person out of a cult is one thing...
Getting the cult out of the person is another" **Ex-cult member**

Withdrawal symptoms

For those who are fortunate enough to leave a cult, there then begins a difficult rehabilitation period. This typically takes a year or more. During this time the ex-member experiences a variety of symptoms of withdrawal. These symptoms include the following:

- insomnia
- amnesia
- delusions
- emotional outbursts
- floating in and out of altered states of consciousness
- guilt
- sexual dysfunction
- hallucinations
- confusion
- disorientation
- abnormal weight gain/loss
- fear of the cult group
- suicidal tendencies.

Without adequate advice and information to help the ex-member understand that experiencing these symptoms is normal, their rehabilitation is likely to be prolonged for an indefinite period. [1]

What they need

When an ex-cult member has escaped from a cult, life is difficult for many reasons. Not only is the recovery long and painful, but there are needs that an ex-member has. These needs include the following:

- to feel normal
- to be understood
- to receive unconditional love and support from family and friends
- to talk to sympathetic ears
- to be able to ask questions and have them answered
- to be free to doubt
- to be recognised as an independent free-thinking individuals again
- to feel worthwhile

1. See 'Information Disease' Conway & Siegelman, Science Digest, Jan 1982 (USA) for more information on this topic.

- to have a 'safe' place to live at little or no cost
- to feel secure
- to feel encouraged to see some positive learning from the otherwise negative experience
- to be able to set the pace of their own rehabilitation
- to learn your language while you learn theirs
- to feel accepted
- to be free to talk about anything good that may have arisen from the cult experience
- to feel trusted
- to be free to talk about the decent people they met in the cult
- to feel wanted
- to have an opportunity to do manual work to give their minds a rest
- to be respected.

Questioning

Not only does an ex-cult member face a long period of withdrawal and have many needs, as we have already seen, but there are many questions that are likely to float around in his mind. The ex-member is likely to be most appreciative of both a sympathetic ear and someone who feels comfortable discussing these issues.

Some of the questions are likely to include the following:

- What happened to me?
- Who can I trust?
- What can I believe?
- How could the other cult members do that to me?
- Who is God?

- Where can I get help?
- How long will it take for me to feel normal again?
- Who will ever understand?
- Will I ever fully recover?
- Why did God not stop the cult from recruiting me?
- Why do I feel so lousy and confused?
- Was the group really wrong?
- How do I get a job?
- What's been happening in the world?
- Who is the current Prime Minister?
- If I knew how to get a job, what kind of job should I get?
- What can I do about friends and family that I have left behind in the cult?
- Why is society not protected from cults?
- What can I say to my old friends to explain where I have been?
- Why didn't anyone warn me?
- What do I put on my CV (résumé)?

Family needs

It is a marvellous relief for a family and for their friends when a loved one is able to break free from a cult, but considering that the ex-member now faces many months of withdrawal, the family's difficulties are not yet over. New problems and stresses emerge for the family to contend with whilst they support the recovering ex-cult member.

Through this period the family has certain difficulties that are as follows:

Difficulty: Fear of talking to the ex-cult member about life in the cult because it might be too stressful for him.

Solution: He may also be scared of talking to the family for the same reason so it is better to discuss it with him, but only if he agrees and only for as long as he agrees.

Difficulty: Fear that if he speaks favourably about some of the cult members, it might mean that he is considering going back into the cult.

Solution: Decent people become victims of cults daily. It is normal for an ex-cult member to speak fondly of some of them and to feel great sorrow because of their continuing exploitation by the cult.

Difficulty: Fear of saying the wrong thing that might be hurtful to the ex-cult member.

Solution: Be open but gentle with him and let him determine whether or not an issue should be discussed at any point in time. Siblings may still feel left out and neglected. Try to be involved with them in their lives too and discuss any difficulties that have arisen.

Difficulty: Family members feel exhausted and have been running on adrenaline for too long.

Solution: Consider having a family holiday with the ex-cult member.

DOS AND DON'TS: for families and friends of recovering ex-cult members

The Dos

Do express love clearly.

Do things together as a family.

Do show that no blame is attached to the ex-member.

Do encourage simple decision-making, eg: asking the ex-member to choose a meal, video, etc.

Do realise that full healing usually takes a lot of time, love and understanding.

Do talk about the cult when the ex-member wants to do so.

Do screen out phone calls and mail from the cult with the ex-member's approval.

Do accompany the ex-cult member initially, when outside the home.

The Don'ts

Do not pressure the ex-member to go back to work or study too soon.

Do not be scared of discussing your feelings.

Do not be suffocatingly protective.

Do not blame the ex-member for being involved in the cult.

Do not assume the cult will not try to take the ex-member back.

Do not assume that he will not make a complete recovery.

Chapter 6

What can we do?

"The only thing necessary for the triumph of evil is for good men to do nothing." **Edmund Burke**

HOW TO AVOID BEING RECRUITED

A checklist of cult techniques

Cults use many ploys to recruit the unsuspecting. In order to offer practical advice about how to avoid being recruited by a cult, the following is a checklist of typical things that cults do. Remember that it is not proof that you are dealing with a cult or cult-recruiter. However, perhaps the list will provoke people to be careful and at least get a second opinion.

Beware of:

★ People that try to recruit you to go to a meeting through the use of guilt. *Guilt induced by others is rarely a productive emotion. Examples of this are "I thought you were my friend" and "Don't you care about starving people?"*

★ People with easy answers or solutions to world problems. *While some easy answers can be found, things may not be as they initially appear.*

★ People with invitations to free meals and/or lectures, where the objectives are not clearly stated. *There may be a hidden agenda.*

★ People who pressure you because "everyone else is doing it". *'Everyone else' could be making a mistake.*

★ People who are vague or evasive about answering questions when promoting courses, meetings or other gatherings. *There could be a hidden agenda.*

★ People using hypnosis without formal mental-health training and accountability. *Hypnosis is a controversial and powerful technique that can be used for the benefit of the hypnotist and not the client.*

★ People offering 'meditation' or 'relaxation'

35

methods that involve sitting listening to someone guiding you through an 'experience' that may be a disguise for hypnosis. *Cults use many disguises for hypnosis.*

★ People who are excessively or inappropriately friendly the first time you meet them and want to talk to you about going to a meeting, course or other gathering. *There could be a hidden agenda.*

★ Invitations to seminars having nebulous goals. *There could be a hidden agenda.*

★ Groups that are exclusive and elitist. *This could lead to isolating you from the outside world and rational points of reference.*

★ People, groups and courses where you have a gut feeling something is wrong. *You may well be right. Too many people have ignored such feelings when con-* *fronted by a cult or cult-recruiter and later regretted not acting on the feelings.*

★ Courses that demand no talking to people sitting on either side of you. *Cults often forbid side-talking to stop you from realising that other people on your course are equally puzzled or concerned about an issue.*

★ Courses where you are frowned upon for taking prescribed drugs. *It is believed that some drugs may interfere with a cult's ability to psychologically coerce and control an individual.*

★ Courses with no course outline, where they tell you that to have one would be "like reading the last page of an exciting book—it would spoil it for you". *If you knew exactly what was to occur on the course, you might not wish to participate and with good reason.*

What can we do to protect ourselves?

1. BE BETTER INFORMED.
Read books about cults and look for articles in the media on the topic.

2. BE ALERT.
To local cult-related issues.

3. WARN YOUR COMMUNITY, company or local religious institution about the general dangers of cults, or invite a specialist cult critic to do so.

4. ADVISE YOUR LOCAL MEDIA, clergy, schools, professional groups and politicians about specific cults operating in your area.

5. PLACE BOOKS about the problems posed by cults in libraries (see booklist).

6. HELP cult awareness organisations.

★ Courses where very little sleep is allowed because of the long hours each day. *Sleep deprivation is a common ploy used by cults to fatigue people and make them less able to critically evaluate what is happening to them.*

★ Courses where questioning is inhibited or prohibited. *If someone realises that the course is manipulative, or problematic in some other way, this is a way of preventing that information reaching the other participants.*

★ Courses in locations where there is no adequate ventilation. *A lack of fresh air in a cult-run course can help to fatigue people and make them less critically able.*

★ Courses where there are no or few breaks for food. *Interfering with the normal breaks one would expect for food. It disrupts natural rhythms and helps to fatigue people too.*

★ Courses where there are no or restricted bathroom breaks. *The discomfort felt can assist a cult in fatiguing an individual and help to build up dependency on the group.*

★ Courses where you are never or rarely allowed to talk to another new person. *This also is to stop you from realising that other people on your course are equally puzzled or concerned about an issue.*

★ Courses where you are not supposed to wear a watch. *It can be very disorientating to not know the time of day or how much time has elapsed.*

★ Courses where you have to sit in a new seat after each break. *If someone has been thrown out of the class during the break, perhaps because they have seen through the tactics being employed, the person is less likely to be missed because whoever was sitting on either side of the person before the break would not be doing so after the break.*

★ Courses where the breaks are few and far between, and which start early, and finish late. *Cults often do this to fatigue the participants.*

★ Courses that require personal, confidential details about your life and/or goals ahead of taking the course. *This information could be used later to manipulate you to co-operate with the cult or to silence a potential critic.*

★ Courses in locations where there are no windows or where the windows have been covered by cardboard, brown paper or very heavy drapes, so that no outside light can penetrate into the room. *Cults use this technique, along with forbidding the wearing of watches, to prevent people from guessing the time of day through not being able to see if it is even light or dark outside. It helps to disorientate people.*

★ Giving money to smiling people, who block your path whilst aggressively claiming to represent charities and using guilt to make you donate. *Millions of pounds are generated by cults in this way.*

★ Meetings of groups you have never heard of that occur in prestigious locations. *Many cults use the credibility of an institution to lend credibility to themselves. Many people naively assume that any organisation renting space from a library, hotel, university or church must be OK, and that it would not be allowed to rent the space if it was not equally reputable. Sadly, this is all too often not the case.*

★ Buying paintings, cacti, ornaments etc. being sold door to door by people representing charities you have never heard of. *Most cults find it easy to obtain charitable status, presumably to give themselves credibility and avoid paying taxes.*

RECOMMENDED READING LIST

Releasing the Bonds **Steven Hassan** (Freedom of Mind Press)

Combatting Cult Mind Control **Steven Hassan** (Park Street Press)

Moonwebs **Josh Freed** (Virgo Publishing)

Snapping **Flo Conway & Jim Siegelman** (Stillpoint Press)

Captive Hearts, Captive Minds **Madeleine Tobias & Janja Lalich** (Hunter House)

Cults in our Midst **Margaret Singer with Janja Lalich** (Jossey Bass)

Influence **Robert Cialdini** (Harper Collins)

The Secret World of Cults **Jean Ritchie** (Angus & Robertson)

Thought Reform and the Psychology of Totalism **Robert Lifton** (University of North Carolina Press)

Churches that Abuse **Ronald Enroth** (Zondervan)

Cults:What Parents Should Know **Joan Ross with Michael Langone** (Lyle Stuart Books)

Many of the above books and other publications are available from:
Cult Information Centre,
BCM CULTS,London WC1N 3XX
Tel: 0845 4500 868
and from their website: www.cultinformation.org.uk

Resisting manipulation

Adapted from 'Resisting Mind Control' by Susan M. Anderson and Philip G. Zimbardo, USA Today 1980

Be on the alert
Going passively along 'on automatic' is often our worst enemy. When we habitually take simple assumptions for granted in a setting, we fail to check out the reality.
• Actively monitor social interactions. Practice thinking ahead, anticipating what will come next, checking discrepancies and noting how you feel about them.
• Be willing to disobey simple situational rules when you feel you should. Don't be afraid of causing a scene in such a situation. Never do anything you don't believe just to appear normal or to get someone off your back.
• At the very least, try to get more information so you can carefully consider the consequences of saying "no" to something that could turn out essentially 'good' (could you return in a week or a year and say "yes"?), or of saying "yes" to something that could turn out essentially 'bad' (could you lose your money, pride, or life?).

Beware of some 'experts'
Millions of people are subjected to stress and intimidation in the presence of those whom society has termed expert. Unscrupulous car mechanics, for example, often persuade people to buy parts or services they don't need. It is important to be assertive.
• Practice 'seeing through' programmed responses to authority. Pay attention to the social roles you and others play, including such subtle indicators as cloth-ing—the business suit, repairman's uni-form, etc..
• Don't assume, just because someone claims to be or is described as an expert, that he is or that his advice is reliable.
• To the extent that it seems possible, refuse to accept the initial premise that someone else is more powerful, more competent, more in control than you are.
• Be aware of who is controlling whom in social situations, to what end and at what cost.
• State your arguments with conviction if the other person does so.

Retain your sense of self-worth
Learn to retain a sense of self-worth in the face of intimidating circumstances.
• Remember, you might be the only person at the meeting that has seen through the manipulative ploys or the inconsistencies and contradictions.

Exercise your critical faculties
Experienced manipulators try to appear to be just like us. They use familiar terms and phrases in order to influence our attitudes. Attitude change is most effective when it goes unnoticed.
• Learn to spot flattery and overemphasis on mutual interests.
• Beware of requests for 'just one small commitment now', with an open-ended contract for later.
• Never accept vague generalities and inadequate explanations in response to your pleas, questions, or challenges.
• Learn to recognise when a message is actually confused or ambiguous, per-

haps intentionally so, especially if someone suggests "you're just too stupid to understand" or "women get too emotional to think logically."

- Paraphrase other people's thoughts both aloud and to yourself to see if you're understanding clearly.
- Practice generating arguments and counter-arguments as you listen to persuasive messages, to avoid slipping into 'automatic' processing.
- Always seek outside information and criticism before joining a group or making a commitment to invest time, energy or money in some endeavour.
- Train yourself and your family to notice the 'tricks' in deceptive packaging, such as those used in tv commercials.

Don't let a group make you feel awkward

Susceptibility to mind control becomes greater when individuals are forced to focus attention on themselves, making them feel deviant or silly.

- Be sensitive to and avoid situations and people that put you on the spot, making you feel different, awkward, or inadequate.
- Try to focus on what you are doing, rather than on thoughts about yourself. Don't generate negative internal dialogues about yourself, and never accept a chronically negative view from someone else.
- Be willing to look foolish now and then, to accept being 'different' as being 'special' rather than inferior.

Combat Stressful Situations

Many of the most powerfully persuasive appeals are based on making people afraid or anxious.

- No matter what the relationship, avoid getting drawn into unwanted confessions that may later be used against you.
- Avoid making decisions when under stress, particularly in the presence of the person who has made you feel stressed in the first place. Tell them you'll decide tomorrow.
- As you feel yourself becoming uncomfortable, begin taking slower, deeper breaths to help your body relax.

Look at your real options

Once they have control, the slickest operators then emphasise the victim's freedom of choice, while denigrating the alternatives. The newly persuaded person chooses 'freely' while the influencer bolsters his or her decision.

- Be wary of people who overemphasise how free you are to choose—but only from among the options they offer. Electing to have a red vacuum cleaner over a green one is not the same as deciding whether you actually need a new vacuum cleaner in the first place.
- Test the limits of your options by selecting 'none of the above' or by proposing unexpected alternatives, at least tentatively, especially when you create them yourself and think they are better.
- Beware of people using 'reverse psychology' against you. It is the equivalent of a salesman saying "Excuse me for saying so, but this is quite an exclusive line. You may not be able to afford it." Try agreeing with him by saying, "You're right, that merchandise is too expensive" and note his reaction. If he starts pushing in the opposite direction or simply looks befuddled, you may have uncovered a hidden agenda.

LEGAL ISSUES

Typical questions

Q: I have been mentally/physically injured by a cult. Can the law help in any way?

If you have been injured by a cult, whether physically or mentally, you can bring a court case seeking financial compensation for your injuries. Lawyers call this sort of compensation 'damages'. Your chances of success will depend on the individual facts of your case. The law imposes a limit on the amount of time that may pass between an injury being inflicted and a court case being brought. It is therefore important to seek professional advice at the earliest opportunity, as legal actions may be disadvantaged or even defeated by delay.

Q: I have lost money to a cult. Can the law help in any way?

You may bring a court action against a cult to seek return of money used for courses etc or property given to it. Your action could be dismissed (thrown out) if the court feels that you have waited too long before you make a claim. It is therefore important to take professional advice at the earliest possible opportunity.

Q: I am concerned about giving money via a will or other means to a child or relative involved in a cult. What should I do?

There are many ways that you can help someone while preventing money and gifts from falling into the wrong hands. The most well-known way of doing this is to use a 'trust'. A trust is a legal device which normally involves two responsible adults ('the trustees') looking after your gift or bequest, and either paying the income it generates to the child or spending the money on items which will be of benefit to the child, for example on school or university fees. A trust need not be complex; it can be set up very simply either by a will or by a deed created during one's lifetime. It is important to seek professional advice, but such advice need not be expensive.

Q: I am concerned that a family member is giving all their money to a cult while they don't know what they are doing. What can I do?

This is a complex legal issue. The law assumes that adults can dispose of property however they wish, even if they wish to give all their money to non-conventional organisations. You will only be able to use the law to prevent this if the person is not deemed to be mentally capable of managing their own affairs, that is, if the person does not know that they are giving money away or is not capable of understanding how it will be used. If the court finds that a person is not capable of managing their own affairs, then it may appoint someone known as a 'receiver' to step in and manage that person's affairs. To prove to the court that someone is not mentally capable will normally require evidence from a doctor or psychologist.

Q: A member of my family has left a will and the beneficiary is a cult. What can I do?

The law starts from the position that an adult is free to dispose of his property however he sees fit. Wills made under duress or by a person who is not mentally capable of managing their own affairs can be set aside. If a person who was dependent on the deceased has not been provided for in a will ,then they may be able to make a claim against the deceased's property. Making such a claim need not be complicated, but each case is different and must be assessed on its own merits. Legal advice should be sought as soon as possible, as there are time limits within which such claims must be made.

Q: My partner/spouse is a member of a cult and I am worried about my children. What can I do?

Courts are keen to protect children from harm wherever possible. If this issue arises during a divorce or separation, then you should inform the lawyer who is acting for you. If you are not thinking about divorce or separation, you should seek the advice of a lawyer specialising in family law matters.

General points

These suggestions cannot take the place of comprehensive legal advice. The facts of each case will always have a major impact on what can or cannot be done. The sooner legal advice is sought, the more likely it is to be effective, particularly as there are strict deadlines for dealing with certain types of problem. If you think you might benefit from legal advice, the Cult Information Centre can put you in touch with a suitable solicitor. Alternatively, the Law Society or your local Citizens Advice Bureau may be able to recommend a firm to you.

The Cult Information Centre (CIC)

The Cult Information Centre (CIC) is a registered charity. Its registered charity number is 1012914. It has been in operation since 1987.

CIC's concerns

CIC is concerned about deceptive and psychologically manipulative methods used by cults to recruit and indoctrinate unsuspecting members of society. CIC believes that these methods present a threat to the well-being of the individual and the family. Consequently CIC sees the need for gathering and disseminating accurate information on cultism and aims to meet that need.

International network

CIC has established links with an international network of reliable cult-aware contacts, particularly in the western world. This network of people, knowledgeable in cultism, comprises individuals from a wide variety of disciplines and includes other specialists in cultism, mental health professionals, clergy, relatives of current members and ex-cult members. These contacts have proved invaluable to those with loved ones in a cult in a foreign land.

What does CIC do ?

★ PUBLIC EDUCATION
CIC gives preventative educational talks to schools, colleges, universities, churches, clubs and corporations.

★ MEDIA INTERVIEWS
CIC helps the media with interviews to further disseminate information on cultism.

★ CORPORATE CONSULTING
CIC acts as a consultant to corporations facing, or anticipating the potential for, cult related problems.

★ FAMILY ASSISTANCE
CIC offers assistance and support for families who have lost a loved one to a cult.

★ EX-CULT MEMBERS SUPPORT
CIC offers information and support to ex-cult members who usually experience symptoms of cult withdrawal for a year or more after leaving a cult.

★ RESEARCH ASSISTANCE
CIC assists students and other researchers with bibliographies and other information for projects, academic papers and books.

★ INFORMATION SERVICE
CIC provides information to the general public when questions are asked about a particular group's possible connection with a cult.

About the author

Ian Haworth founded the 'Cult Information Centre' in the UK in 1987 but has been an educator working full-time specialising in speaking and writing about the dangers of cults since 1979. After breaking away from a cult in Canada in 1978, he experienced 11 months of symptoms of withdrawal. Over the years he has acted as a consultant to the police, law firms, the media, social agencies, religious institutions, educators, mental-health professionals and corporations, and has been an expert witness in cult-related civil and criminal trials in both Canada and the UK. He is a regular contributor to television and radio programmes on the subject of cults.

Further information and advice

Additional information may be obtained from the following location:
Cult Information Centre
BCM CULTS
London
WC1N 3XX
Phone: 0845 4500 868
Website: www.cultinformation.org.uk

The Cult Information Centre (CIC) provides public speakers, counselling for families with a loved one in a cult, support for ex-cult members and corporate consulting for businesses.

CIC is a registered charity (Charity No. 1012914). It also has a national and international network of contacts that can offer further information on the topic of cults.

Suggestions for small group discussion

1. *Read the list of the five marks of a cult on page 12.* What groups can you think of that exhibit some of all of these qualities?

2. Have you or someone you know ever had any experience of cult involvement?

3. Do you think that you are the sort of person who might be recruited by a cult? Why/why not?

Now read the section on page 13 about who the cults target for recruitment.

Does it surprise you that you are more vulnerable than you might think?

4. *Read the list of recruitment techniques on pages 35-38.* You meet a person on the street. What are some of the clues that he/she is trying to recruit you into a cult?

5. How should you react to a cult recruiter who is trying to recruit you on the street?

6. *Read the Diary of a Cult recruitment story on pages 19-22.* Why do you think that the woman was vulnerable to recruitment and manipulation?

7. What mistakes do you think she made as she got involved in the cult?

8. Cult techniques are so powerful that we are always vulnerable to their methods. List times in life, when you might be even more vulnerable than usual.

9. You have been invited to a meeting where you start to recognise that mind-control techniques are being used. List some of the things you might do to combat the pressure you come under. *(see pages 35-39 for some examples)*

10. Imagine you are a friend of the woman in the story. How might you try to help her to leave?

11. You have just realised your best friend is in a cult and is trying to recruit you—how should you respond? *(see chapter 6 for suggestions)*

12. A friend or family member has just left a cult. What practical things can you do to help them cope with the adjustment? *(see chapter 5 for suggestions)*